Holiday Cocktails

Holiday Cocktails

A Connoisseur's Guide to Seasonal Drinks

ELIZABETH WOLF-COHEN

THE LYONS PRESS

A SALAMANDER BOOK

Published in the United States by
The Lyons Press
Guilford, CT 06437
www.lyonspress.com
An imprint of The Globe Pequot Press

ISBN 1-58574-623-1

1 2 3 4 5 6 7 8 9 10

Credits
Project managed by: Stella Caldwell and Charlotte Davies
Editorial assistant: Katherine Edelston
Designed by: The Design Revolution, Sussex, UK
Color reproduction: Global Graphics, Prague, Czech Republic
Printed and bound in Taiwan

Contents

Introduction

Cocktails as we know them have existed from at least the beginning of the nineteenth century. However, it was not until the Prohibition Era of 1920s America that cocktails, mixed alcoholic drinks, really began to take off when they were concocted to make palatable drinks from an assortment of poor quality bootlegged liquors. With the lifting of the alcohol ban in 1933 and the raising of overall standards of liquor, many of the more acceptable recipes were refined, and even more were created. The cocktail boom soon spread around the world and became synonymous with sophistication and glamour.

Cocktails have an enduring appeal and today they are ideal for contemporary lifestyles. Nowadays, people are entertaining at home more than ever, and often more casually. Any occasion on which cocktails are consumed feels like more of a celebration than drinking beer or wine.

Holiday Cocktails provides cocktail recipes for special times of the year, from Valentine's Day to Easter and Thanksgiving. This book shows that cocktails are fun and that it is not always necessary to have an extensive range of drinks. Like many cookery recipes, recipes for cocktails can be modified to suit personal tastes or ingredients that are available. *Holiday Cocktails* provides recipes for classic celebration drinks as well as more recent creations. There are even a few non-alcoholic drinks and cocktails which are equally delicious, and a selection of canapés and finger foods rounds off the book.

Cocktails should stimulate the palate and get the senses buzzing in anticipation of what comes next. Most cocktails are based on a single spirit to which is added a variety of flavorings which complement or contrast to form an individual drink. Spirits are alcohols produced by the process of distillation. Heat separates the components of a liquid or mash and, as they cool, the vapors condense into neutral spirits with little color or flavor. This is then blended with other alcohols or flavorings and left to age (or not), sometimes in wood casks, until the desired flavor is achieved before bottling.

Sometimes two or more spirits are combined in a cocktail and the range of possible additions and mixers is almost endless; everything from distilled wines such as brandy or Cognac, distilled grains such as gin, vodka or whisky (Scotch) to flavored spirits and bitters, liqueurs, sparkling wines, fortified wines, syrup cordials and fruit juices, or even milk, eggs and cream can be added to create a unique drink. The following is a brief guide to the ingredients most frequently used.

Distillations from Wine

Armagnac: a pale, dry fiery brandy coming from the Armagnac region of southwest France.

Brandy: a double-distilled alcohol with a nutty deep gold color coming from its aging in oak barrels.

Cognac: the best known brandy in the world, Cognac comes from the town of Cognac in the Charente region of France and must be made from specific grapes in the area.

Grappa: a clear Italian spirit made from the remains of the grapes from wine production, Grappa is dry and very fiery.

Metaxa: This is a Greek brandy made from black grapes.

Distillations from Grains, Fruits and Plants

Aquavit: a strong Scandinavian spirit, this pure, almost tasteless alcohol is almost 200 per cent proof!

Gin: this popular clear spirit is distilled from barley and rye, then flavored with herbs and spices, most predominantly juniper which gives it its characteristic flavor.

Vodka: this pure, clear, smooth spirit has a neutral taste which makes it perfect as a base for cocktails. It is distilled from a mixture of grains and potatoes.

Whisky: probably the most widely drunk liquor in the world, whisky is produced in many countries. It can be distilled from malted barley or mixed grains (Scotland), barley, wheat, rye or oats (Irish Whisky), corn (Bourbon—King of American whiskies), a 51 per cent rye blend with other grains (rye whisky), or blended straight grain (Canadian Whisky). Whiskies can be made from a single malt or blended and vary in color, strength and flavor; for cocktail mixing, it is not necessary to use the finest, most subtle one.

Eau-de-vies: these colorless brandies are generally fruit flavored; the most famous fruit spirit is probably Calvados, an apple brandy produced in Normandy, France.

Other well-known alcoholic ingredients are:

Rum: a spirit made from the molasses by-product of sugar cane refining; Sake, a Japanese fermented rice spirit; and Tequila, a spirit distilled from the blue agave cactus.

Bitters are produced from herb and root extracts; the most commonly used are Angostura Bitters from Trinidad, Campari from Italy and orange bitters.

Liqueurs: spirits which are flavored with fruits, plants or oils, then sweetened with honey or glucose (sugar). Liqueurs vary in their alcohol content and can be very strong. Their color, flavor and sweetness make them indispensable in cocktail-making. Famous flavors range from Ameretto (almond), Anisette (star anise and fennel), B&B (Benedictine and brandy), Cointreau (Seville oranges and lemons), Curacao (bitter orange from Curacao), Drambuie (Scotch whisky), and the list goes on. Even milk, cream, chocolate and eggs can be added to give texture and flavor.

Fortified Wines such as Madeira, Marsala, Port, Sherry and Vermouth are also used as mixers or sometimes on their own.

Glasses

Choosing a suitable glass for your cocktail can really enhance its appearance. Although there are many styles and shapes of glasses and although there are some classic pairings of glasses and cocktails, such as a dry Martini in a cocktail glass, or an Old-Fashioned in an old-fashioned glass, in general the style and shape of glass used is not really critical. In this book we have indicated a style of glass for each drink, but you may have to substitute as not everyone at home has the selection of a cocktail bar.

However, whatever the glass, it should be spotlessly clean and free from any detergent or odor. When stored upside down, air can be trapped in the bow and can affect the smell and taste of a drink that is later served in it. If glasses have been stored upside down for any length of time, rinse and dry them before using. Colored or heavily patterned glasses can detract from the appearance of a drink. Be sure to choose a glass that will suit the quantity of the drink, especially if it is served on ice.

Types of Traditional Glasses

Cocktail glass: this classic 'V'-shaped glass is also called a Martini glass, but it can be any shape as long as it holds about one half cup / 115 ml liquid.

Old Fashioned: this traditional short tumbler has slightly sloping sides and holds about one cup / 175–225 ml.

Whisky tumbler: similar to an old-fashioned glass, but with straight sides.

Highball: this tall, straight-sided tumbler holds about one and a half cups / 350 ml.

Champagne flute: the shape of glass that is fashioned now is tall, slim and curves out slightly at the rim, but the old-fashioned, saucer-shaped glass is experiencing a revival. Some people complain that the bubbles disappear too quickly and the drink warms; this has never been a problem in my house!

Wine glass or "tulip" glass: many different sizes and styles of this glass are available; they should hold between one half to three quarters of a cup / 115–175 ml.

Brandy balloon: brandy glasses are available in a range of sizes. Although only a small amount is served, the inward curving of the bowl traps the vapor and aroma of the drink and the additional space allows for some swirling to release the perfume.

Punch glass: usually matching a punch bowl, these small, mug-shaped glasses should be heat-proof if used for hot punches. They usually match a large punch bowl.

Liqueur glasses: these small glasses vary tremendously in shape and are used for after dinner liqueurs, not cocktails; as a last resort they can be used as a measure.

Large goblet/balloon or red wine glasses: these glasses vary in size and shape and can be used for almost anything from simple wine spritzers to exotic cocktails. They hold between one and one and three quarters cups / 250–450 ml.

Bar Equipment and Ingredients

Although the right equipment makes preparing cocktails and garnishes a lot easier and looks professional, not much is essential. Most drinks can be made with a small selection of utensils found at home. If you really intend to entertain extensively, it would be worthwhile and fun to invest. The selection below is a basic list.

Measure: in this book, I generally use the term "measure"; this means it doesn't matter what the exact size of the measure is, as long as it remains consistent within the preparation of a drink. The standard bar measure varies between countries, but is usually about 3 tablespoons / 45 ml. If you do not have a standard bar measure, use a shot glass, liqueur glass or an egg cup! Most of the cocktails in this book are made for one serving; for larger amounts use a kitchen measuring cup or jug.

Cocktail shaker: a standard stainless steel cocktail shaker consists of two parts that fit together with an integral strainer. More elaborate silver cocktail shakers are available if you plan on serious home cocktail serving. Alternatively, a wide-necked screw-top jar can be used. To use, add the stipulated ingredients and a scoop of ice to the larger bottom bowl, cover and, depending on the style of the shakes, twist together and hold the two parts together with both hands. Shake vertically and briskly (don't "roll") until the shaker is ice cold and frosty on the outside.

Strainer: a classic bartender's strainer is made of stainless steel; it has springy wire coil around the edge and the flat surface has holes. Another type is a large-headed, spoon-shaped strainer; it is attractive, but sometimes allows extra ice to slip in.

Other useful equipment

The following items are useful, but generally ordinary kitchen equipment can be substituted: mixing glass; long-handled spoon for stirring tall drinks; toothpicks (or cocktail sticks) for decorations; drinking straws; teaspoon and tablespoon; stainless steel vegetable knife; small chopping (or cutting) board for cutting lemons etc.; fruit juicer or squeezer; heatproof glass or measuring cup (jug) to hold hot water in which to rinse spoons used for mixing drinks; clean dish towel and dish cloth; paper towels; corkscrew; bottle opener; closure for sparkling wines; ice bucket; scoop; and drink mat.

Ingredients

There are hundreds of alcohols, but most cocktails can be made with a basic well-stocked home bar. Choose drinks that you will make most frequently, then to keep costs down, buy half or quarter bottles where possible. When a particular brand is specified, for example an orange liqueur, other brands may be substituted.

Most useful alcoholic drinks: gin; vodka; rum (dark and white); brandy; whisky (scotch, rye or bourbon); vermouth (dry and sweet); tequila; at least one orange liqueur such as Curacao, Contreau or Grand Marnier; crème de menthe; Amaretto di Serrano, cherry brandy; apricot brandy; crème de cacao; Tia Maria or Kahlua; and Galliano. Angostura bitters, Campari and orange bitters are also very useful.

Mixers: soda water; ginger ale; tonic water; lemon-lime soda (lemonade); and grenadine.

Other preparations

Cracked ice: put the ice cubes in a plastic freezer bag and twist to close. Bring the bag down sharply on a firm surface, or hit it with a hammer or rolling pin. Alternatively, crack ice cubes in a food processor.

Crushed ice: prepare the same way as cracked ice, but crush more finely. Alternatively, use a blender.

Powdered sugar: briefly grind granulated sugar in a blender or food processor. Powdered sugar will dissolve more quickly and easily than other sugars.

Simple sugar syrup: often called stock syrup, this is frequently used in cocktails, and is easy to make yourself. Stir equal amounts of sugar and water together in a saucepan and bring to a boil without stirring; once syrup boils, do not stir. For a thicker syrup, boil longer. Allow to cool, bottle, then store in a cool, dark place.

Mixing

Cocktail-making is not difficult but following some basic guidelines will make it easier.

- Keep all drinks in a cool place; keep mixers, wines and juices in the fridge.
- Use chilled glasses; to chill quickly, fill with cracked ice for a few minutes. Empty the ice and dry glasses before using. Handle glasses by the stem or base and never put your fingers inside a glass or near a rim.
- A "dash" is the amount released in a quick squirt from a bottle.

• Prepare drinks on a waterproof surface, so water marks and spills will not spoil other surfaces.

• Always add ice to the cocktail shaker, but remember the more ice that is used, the colder the drink will be. Too much ice, especially crushed ice, will dilute the drink. Crushed ice cools a drink more, and more quickly, than cracked ice.

• With few exceptions, always strain cocktails that have been shaken to remove the ice and other solid ingredients which may have been used for flavor.

• Do not put carbonated or fizzy ingredients into a cocktail shaker as they will fizz up and spill over the top.

• For clear ice, use mineral water; tap water can sometimes make cloudy ice cubes. Do not use the same ice in the shaker for different types of drinks because any residual liquid will taint the next drink.

• Generally, clear drinks are stirred gently, while those containing ingredients that will make the drink cloudy, such as fruit juices, cream and egg white, are shaken or mixed in a blender.

• "Shake" means just that; shake sharply, do not "roll" the shaker. Start to add the ingredients by putting the least expensive ingredients in first. That way, if you make a mistake, only the cheapest ingredient is wasted. Add the remaining ingredients with a scoop of ice. Close the shaker tightly and shake firmly and vertically for a few seconds until the shaker is frosty. Open and strain into a chilled glass.

• Wash equipment between preparing different types of drinks.

• Keep a large pitcher or jug of warm water close by for rinsing equipment.

• If serving an elaborately decorated drink with straws, choose a substantial glass or goblet rather than a delicate or narrow-necked glass.

• When serving drinks with lots of ice or frosted rims, add straws for neater drinking.

• Taste is subjective, so if a drink seems strong (or weak) alter the proportion of ingredients, or add other ingredients as you like, to suit your own taste.

Garnishes & Decoration

The appearance of a cocktail is important and any decoration should enhance the drink. With a few cocktails, such as the "Martini", the decoration is an integral part of the recipe, but in most cases it can be varied according to taste and availability.

• Use garnishes to complement a drink's taste and color. In general, "less is more".

• If using fresh fruit, make sure it's ripe and blemish-free as well as carefully sliced. Use a lemon zester or vegetable peeler for long twists of lemon or orange peel.

• All garnishes and decorations should be edible. Small fruits such as raspberries, strawberries, melon balls, grapes, cherries, and pieces of fruit are most suitable.

• Cherries are a popular choice; fresh cherries on their stems are beautiful.

• Strawberries, raspberries, grapes and red currants look stunning when frosted (crystallized). Dip each fruit into a little lightly beaten egg white, then dip into superfine (caster) sugar and set on a plate to dry.

• Vegetable garnishes such as celery sticks, and olives, can be used for savory drinks.

• Fruit Kabits (kebabs) look stunning across the rim of the glass. Skewer grapes on to a toothpick between lemon or orange slices or thread pineapple pieces, grapes and red cherries on to a skewer with mint or basil leaves between pieces of fruit.

• One of the prettiest presentations for cocktails is a frosted rim. Hold a cocktail or martini glass by the stem and rub the rim with a wedge of lemon or lime. Place a layer of salt in a saucer and dip the glass into the salt until the rim is evenly coated; gently shake off any excess. For a sweet trim, substitute superfine (caster) sugar for the salt. For a pink rim, use grenadine.

• Decorative ice cubes can make a talking point. Cut shapes from suitable fruits such as orange, lemon or lime peel, mint or small pieces of fresh fruit. Half-fill an ice cube tray with water and freeze. Dip the chosen decoration in water and place a piece on each ice cube; freeze. Fill the remainder of the cubes with water to cover and freeze until ready to use.

Chapter One
New Year's Eve

Ritz Fizz

Champagne always symbolizes celebration. Traditional at weddings, birthdays and anniversaries, it is most often drunk to bring in the New Year. When preparing champagne-based cocktails using other highly flavored ingredients, alternative sparkling white wines can be substituted.

1 sugar cube
3–4 dashes Angostura bitters
half measure of brandy or cognac
chilled champagne

1. Put the sugar lump into the bottom of a champagne flute or champagne saucer and add 3–4 dashes of bitters to soak into the sugar.
2. Add the brandy to the sugar, then fill the glass with chilled champagne; stir gently.

makes 1 cocktail

Celebratory Mulled Red Wine

Although the origin of the word "mull" is uncertain, it has come to mean "to heat and spice a drink". Ales and wines have been mulled for centuries and each country seems to have its own variation. Rich and warming, mulled wines make an ideal cocktail for a winter celebration.

1 (750ml) bottle red wine
5 fl oz / 150 ml ruby port
3 fl oz / 75 ml brandy
3 fl oz / 75 ml triple sec
2 cinnamon sticks
4 whole cloves
4 allspice berries
1 bay leaf
2 tablespoons brown sugar, or to taste
2 oranges and 2 lemons, sliced, to decorate

1. Put the wine, port, brandy, triple sec, spices and sugar in a saucepan and bring to a simmer over a low heat; do not allow to boil. Remove from the heat and allow to stand 15–20 minutes for the flavors to blend.
2. Pour into a heated punch bowl and add the sliced lemons and oranges. Ladle into punch glasses making sure each serving has a slice of orange or lemon.

serves 6–8

Fraise Royal

This deliciously fresh cocktail can't fail to impress. Use one of those "mini" food choppers to puree the strawberries or use a blender to puree a larger quantity. If you are just indulging yourself, mash the strawberries with a fork.

2 fresh ripe strawberries, plus 1 extra to decorate
1–2 teaspoons Crème de Fraise (strawberry liqueur)
chilled champagne

1. Remove the stems from the two strawberries and cut into quarters. Put into a "mini" food chopper or processor with 1–2 teaspoons of the liqueur and process until smooth, or process a larger quantity all at once in a blender. Alternatively, mash the strawberries and liqueur in a small bowl with a fork.
2. Spoon the puree into a champagne flute and top with the chilled champagne.
3. Using a sharp knife, make a slit from the bottom about three-quarters of the way to the stem end of the strawberry, but do not cut in half. To decorate, slide the strawberry onto the edge of the glass.

makes 1 cocktail

Harvey Wallbanger

Because of its neutral character, its lack of smell and flavor, vodka makes a popular base for many cocktails. Its manufacturing process removes many chemical impurities, producing a cleaner, more pure spirit. So although it has a high alcohol content, it is slightly "kinder" to the body as it produces fewer undesirable after-effects than other drinks.

The story goes that a Californian "surfer king" named Harvey won a big prize and went on a celebration binge, banging his surfboard against the wall as he staggered from bar to bar after drinking this delicious, power-packed cocktail. This is basically the classic "Screwdriver" plus the Italian herb-based liqueur, Galliano.

cracked ice
1 measure vodka
freshly squeezed orange juice
half measure Galliano
orange slice, to decorate

1. Half-fill a highball or beer glass with cracked ice. Pour in the orange juice until the glass is three-quarters full. Add the vodka and stir gently to mix.
2. Using a teaspoon held upside down against the edge of the glass, gently pour the Galliano over the spoon so that it spreads and floats over the surface; do not stir.
3. Using a sharp knife, make a slit from the edge to below the center of the orange slice. Slide over the edge of the glass to decorate.

makes 1 cocktail

Chapter Two
Valentine's Day

Love Hearts

This romantic cocktail gets its lovely pink color from the non-alcoholic rose syrup. If you prefer a stronger alcoholic content, substitute grenadine.

1 measure Kirsch
2 measures dry vermouth
1 teaspoon sirop de rose
rose petals or fresh cherry, to decorate

1. Put the Kirsch and vermouth into a goblet and add the sirop de rose; stir gently.
2. If you like, decorate with a few fresh rose petals or a fresh cherry.

makes 2 cocktails

Justine

The origins of the name Justine are unknown, but if the cocktail resembles her she would have been a smooth, seductive and sophisticated lady.

2 measures vodka
1 measure crème de noyau
1 measure Kirsch
2–3 dashes of orgeat syrup or Amaretto
2 measures whipping cream
crushed ice

1. Put the vodka, crème de noyau, Kirsch, orgeat syrup or Amaretto and cream into a cocktail shaker with plenty of ice.
2. Cover and shake vertically until the shaker is frosty; strain into a chilled Martini glass.

makes 1 cocktail

Valentine's Cup

This deep violet colored cocktail is the perfect choice for Valentine's night. A combination of vodka, orange liqueurs and cranberry juice, the addition of the old-fashioned French liqueur, Parfait amour, adds a sweet almond flavor as well as its passionate violet color.

For the special occasion, make heart-shaped ice cubes or freeze small round cubes with crystallized violets in the middle. Alternatively, tint the ice cubes with a cherry or blackcurrant drink—there are not too many occasions when you can go so over the top!

1 measure Parfait amour
1 tablespoon vodka
1 tablespoon blue curacao
1 tablespoon orange curacao
1/4 cup / 60 ml cranberry juice
crushed ice
novelty ice cubes, as above (optional)

1. Put the Parfait amour, vodka, curacao and cranberry juice in a cocktail shaker with plenty of ice.
2. Cover and shake vertically until the shaker is frosty; strain over novelty ice cubes, if you like, or ice or crushed ice, into a Martini or tulip-shaped glass.

makes 1 cocktail

First Night

This brandy-based drink has a hint of coffee flavor and a smooth creamy finish. It isn't necessary to use the best brandy in this cocktail; a younger, less expensive brandy can be successfully substituted. Van der Hum is a South African herb and plant-based liqueur; substitute Benedictine if you can't find it.

2 measures brandy
1 measure Van der Hum or Benedictine
1 measure Tia Maria
1 teaspoon whipping cream
crushed ice

1. Put the brandy, Van der Hum, Tia Maria and cream into a cocktail shaker with plenty of ice.
2. Cover and shake vertically until the shaker is frosty; strain into a chilled Martini glass.

makes 1 cocktail

Chapter Three

St. Patrick's Day

Irish Cocktail

It is thought that the Irish were the first distillers of drinkable spirit, so it is probably true that Irish whisky was the first whisky. A mention of a powerful beverage at a feast near Bushmills is found in the ancient Books of Leinster. It was probably brought back to England with Henry II after his troops discovered the delights of these pioneer distillers. It was probably even later when it crossed the sea to Scotland. Irish whisky is distilled three times in place of Scotch's twice, and the single distillation of many North American whiskies; it has a somewhat light, refined and pleasant taste.

This luscious green cocktail is as green and soft as the Irish landscape. The fresh mintiness of crème de menthe and the herby overtones of the green Chartreuse combine to make the perfect cocktail.

1 measure Irish whisky
6 dashes crème de menthe
3 dashes green Chartreuse
ice cubes
green and red glace cherries, to decorate
** (optional)**

1. Pour the whisky, crème de menthe and Chartreuse into a cocktail shaker with a scoop of ice cubes.
2. Cover and shake vigorously until the shaker is frosty; strain into a cocktail glass. If you like, thread a red and green cherry onto a cocktail stick and rest on the edge of the glass.

makes 1 cocktail

Frozen Irish Coffee

The story goes that Irish coffee was invented by Joe Sheridan, head chef at Shannon Airport, in the early days of transatlantic air travel when Shannon was a refuelling stopover. This frozen version pulls out all the stops and adds the richness of Bailey's chocolate and cream liqueur, crème de café and ice cream—no refuelling necessary!

1 $^1/_3$ measures Irish whisky
1 measure Bailey's chocolate and cream liqueur
$^1/_2$ measure crème de café
1 scoop good quality vanilla ice cream
1 scoop good quality coffee ice cream
cocoa powder and chocolate sticks, to decorate
   (optional)

1. Put the whisky, chocolate and cream liqueur, crème de café and ice creams into a blender with about $^1/_2$ scoop of crushed ice and blend on high until frothy.
2. Pour into a large stemmed goblet and, if you like, dust with cocoa and garnish with the chocolate sticks.

makes 1 cocktail

Green Pixie

This delightful, slightly sparkling "long drink" is based on peach schnapps. Schnapps has become a generic term for any clear, strong, spirit flavored with any kind of fruit, herbs, or even spices such as caraway.

In recent years, many herbal fruit drinks have come on to the market; use a complementary flavor or one with similar fruit overtones in the cocktail.

ice cubes
1 ¹/₂ measures peach schnapps
1 measure melon liqueur
¹/₂ measure blue curacao
¹/₂ cup / 125 ml Aqualibra or similar herbal fruit drink
melon balls, to decorate (optional)

1. Half fill a highball glass or tumbler with ice cubes. Pour over the peach schnapps, melon liqueur and blue curacao.
2. Top with the Aqualibra and, if you like, thread 2–3 melon balls on to a cocktail stick and rest on the edge of the glass to decorate.

makes 1 cocktail

Whisky

This whisky based drink is a classic. The history of whisky is long and fraught with contradictions; but whether it is Irish, Scotch or American, it makes a good base for a cocktail.

Unless drinking Scotch (whisky) straight, it is not necessary to use an expensive single malt whisky; use a blended whisky for this sophisticated cocktail.

1 sugar lump or 1 teaspoon superfine (caster) sugar
1–2 dashes Angostura bitters
2–3 ice cubes
1 measure blended whisky
1 orange slice and a glace cherry, to decorate

1. Drop the sugar lump or sugar into an "old fashioned" glass or short tumbler. Add 1–2 dashes Angostura bitters and allow to soak into the sugar. Crush sugar lump or stir to dissolve.
2. Add 2–3 ice cubes and stir to coat. Pour over the whisky and stir gently.
3. Using a sharp knife, make a slit in the orange from the rind to just below the center and another small slit in the bottom end of the cherry. Slide each on to the edge of the glass to decorate.

makes 1 cocktail

Chapter Four
Easter

Margarita

Margarita, so called after the Mexican love of a wild west bar tender, is probably the most famous tequila-based cocktail. Tequila is made from the agave, a kind of Mexican cactus. Its juice is fermented and double-distilled to produce a very potent, clear spirit. For the export market, it is then aged in casks to achieve its famous gold color.

Originally a powerful mix of tequila, lime juice and sugar syrup, the addition of orange liqueur and a salted glass rim is a relatively modern invention.

2 measures tequila
1 ¹/₂ measures freshly squeezed lime juice
1–2 tablespoons orange liqueur, according to taste
4 cubes ice, crushed

1. Put the tequila, lime juice and orange liqueur into a cocktail shaker with the crushed ice.
2. Cover and shake vertically until the shaker is frosty; pour into a salted, frosted cocktail or Martini glass.

Tip: to decorate, chill a cocktail or Martini glass in the freezer until frosty. Just before serving, rub the rim with a cut lime-half and dip into salt, twisting gently to coat the rim.

makes 1 cocktail

Egg Nog

This brand and rum-based drink is creamy and sweet and deceptively potent. You can use a milk shake mixer to prepare two or more servings together, but a cocktail shaker has more style.

1 measure brandy
1 measure dark rum
1 egg, lightly beaten
1 tablespoon sugar syrup, or to taste
2 measures cold milk
freshly grated nutmeg, to decorate

1. Put the brandy, rum, egg and sugar syrup into a cocktail shaker with a scoop of crushed ice.
2. Cover and shake vertically until the shaker is frosty. Strain into a goblet or red wine glass and stir in the milk. If you like, sprinkle with a little nutmeg, to decorate.

makes 1 cocktail

Cherry Blossom

This brandy-based cocktail makes an ideal springtime cocktail for a special occasion or holiday, such as Easter. The cherry brandy echoes the cherry blossom of the season.

2 measures brandy
3 measures cherry brandy
dash of orange curacao
dash of grenadine
dash of lemon juice

1. Put the brandies, curacao, grenadine and lemon juice in a cocktail shaker with plenty of ice.
2. Cover and shake vertically until the shaker is frosty; strain into a goblet or red wine glass.

makes 1 cocktail

Barbara

The origin of this vodka-based cocktail's name is untraceable, but like the drink, she must have been a creamy, sweet lady.

2 measures vodka
1 measure crème de cacao
1 measure light (single) cream
freshly grated nutmeg, to decorate

1. Put the vodka, crème de cacao and light cream into a cocktail shaker with a scoop of crushed ice.
2. Cover and shake vertically until the shaker is frosty. Strain into a Martini or cocktail glass. If you like, sprinkle a little freshly grated nutmeg on top, to decorate.

makes 1 cocktail

Chapter Five
Father's Day

Ginger Square

This combination of whisky and ginger ale is a popular classic. When made with Canadian whisky, it is called Canadian Ginger and in the US a similar combination of rye whisky and ginger ale is simply called "rye and ginger".

3–4 ice cubes
1 ¹/₂ measures blended Scotch or American whisky
¹/₂ cup–³/₄ cup / 125–200 ml ginger ale, for topping up

1. Half fill a highball or tumbler with ice cubes. Pour in the whisky and top up with the ginger ale. If you like, add extra ice.

Makes 1 cocktail

Dandy

Rye, the second most important American whiskey after Bourbon, can be made anywhere, but the mash must contain a minimum of 51 per cent rye. Rye is slightly harsher than Bourbon and makes a good "mixing" spirit; in this case, the sweetness of Dubonnet softens it just enough.

1 measure rye whiskey
1 measure Dubonnet
dash or 2 of Angostura bitters
3 dashes Cointreau

1. Stir the rye and Dubonnet with a dash or two of bitters and 3 dashes Cointreau.
2. Pour into a Martini or cocktail glass.

makes 1 cocktail

Rusty Nail

This Scotch whisky-based cocktail is the perfect man's cocktail—straight, strong and with a soft, subtle edge and just a hint of sharpness.

3–4 ice cubes
2 measures Scotch whisky
1 measure Drambuie
twist of lemon peel

1. Put the ice cubes into a good-sized tumbler; pour in the Scotch whisky and Drambuie.
2. Rub the edge of the glass with a twist of lemon peel and drop into the glass; serve immediately.

makes 1 cocktail

Sidecar

This mixture of Cognac or brandy with Cointreau and lemon juice is a man's cocktail. Named after an eccentric gentleman who used to arrive at Harry's New York Bar in Paris in the sidecar of a chauffeur driven motorcycle, this remains a classic.

1 measure Cognac or brandy
$^1/_2$ measure Cointreau
$^1/_2$ measure freshly squeezed lemon juice
3 ice cubes, cracked

1. Put the Cognac or brandy, Cointreau, lemon juice and ice into a cocktail shaker.
2. Cover and shake until the shaker is frosty; strain into a Martini or cocktail glass.

makes 1 cocktail

Chapter Six
Fourth of July

American Beauty

Why not celebrate the Fourth of July with this unusual brandy-based cocktail. Be sure to use white crème de menthe or the color will be muddy and unattractive. If you like a strong brandy flavor, use an extra half measure of brandy.

1 measure brandy
1 measure dry vermouth
1 measure white crème de menthe
1 measure freshly squeezed orange juice
ice cubes
$1/2$ measure of tawny port

1. Put the brandy, vermouth, crème de menthe and orange juice in a cocktail shaker with a scoop of ice.
2. Cover and shake vertically until the shaker is frosty; strain into a goblet or cocktail glass and slowly pour in the port.

makes 1 cocktail

Bronx Cocktail

There are so many gin-based cocktails, but this classic continues to please. The addition of both sweet and dry vermouth to the gin and orange gives a slightly herby, yet sweet edge.

2 measures gin
1 measure freshly
squeezed orange juice
1 teaspoon dry vermouth
1 teaspoon sweet vermouth
ice cubes
cracked ice, to serve
orange peel or twist, to
  decorate (optional)

1. Put the gin, orange juice and vermouths into a cocktail shaker with a scoop of ice.
2. Cover and shake vertically. Strain into a tall goblet or highball glass half-filled with cracked ice. If you like, decorate with an orange peel or twist.

makes 1 cocktail

Long Island Iced Tea

This is not the traditional iced tea enjoyed by families on hot summer days in the back yard. This is a vodka-based cocktail with a serious kick—a long drink with long-lasting effects.

1 measure vodka
1 measure light rum
1 measure tequila
1 measure gin
$^1/_2$ measure triple sec
1 measure freshly squeezed lemon juice
2 teaspoons superfine (caster) sugar
$^1/_3$–$^1/_2$ cup / 90–125 ml cold cola
ice cubes
lemon twist and sprig of mint to decorate

1. Put the vodka, rum, tequila, gin, triple sec, lemon juice and sugar in a cocktail shaker with a scoop of ice.
2. Cover and shake vertically until the shaker is frosty. Strain the mixture into a highball glass or tumbler half-filled with ice cubes and add the cola; stir gently. If you like, decorate with a lemon twist and a sprig of mint.

makes 1 cocktail

Whip

Pastis is a blend of herbal ingredients, but the principal flavor is anis (aniseed) with a hint of liquorice. Pastis came into its own after absinthe was banned in France. Its addition to this brandy-based drink gives a cooling edge to this sophisticated cocktail.

1 measure brandy
1 measure Pastis
1 measure dry vermouth
1 measure curacao

1. Put the brandy, pastis, vermouth and curacao into a cocktail shaker with a scoop of ice.
2. Cover and shake vertically until the shaker is frosty. Strain into a Martini or cocktail glass.

makes 1 cocktail

Chapter Seven
Summer Days

Coconut Daiquiri

Although the origin of Daiquiri was a simple mixture of
lightly sweetened rum and lime juice, the Daiquiri has
become a base for more and more elaborate and exotic
mixtures. Frozen Daiquiri can be made by adding crushed
ice, fresh fruit and whizzing in a blender to form a frothy icy
drink.

1 measure white rum
2 measures coconut liqueur
4 measures freshly squeezed lime juice
dash of egg white
ice cubes

1. Put the rum, coconut liqueur, lime juice and egg white into a
cocktail shaker with a scoop of ice.
2. Cover and shake vertically until the shaker is frosty; strain
into a goblet.

makes 1 cocktail

Trinidad Punch

This delicious cocktail has those characteristic Caribbean flavors of rum and lime and really does pack a punch.

3 measures dark rum
2 measures freshly squeezed lime juice
1 teaspoon sugar syrup or superfine (caster) sugar
2–3 dashes Angostura bitters
ice cubes
lemon peel and grated nutmeg, to decorate (optional)

1. Put the rum, lime juice, sugar syrup or sugar and the Angostura bitters into a cocktail shaker with a scoop of ice.
2. Cover and shake vertically until the shaker is frosty. Strain into a large goblet half-filled with ice cubes. If you like, garnish with a twist of lemon peel and dust with nutmeg.

Tip: use a whole nutmeg and a small-holed grater to grate a little nutmeg over the top. This has a wonderful and evocative aroma.

makes 1 cocktail

Cool Green Haze

Punches were brought back to England in the 17th Century after the British captured the island of Jamaica from Spain and, of course, rum was the favored spirit base. By the 18th and 19th centuries, punches were often drunk as an accompaniment to a meal, as we would drink water today—hence the large, ornate punch bowls featured on many tables as center pieces.

Punches are made from a base spirit such as rum or brandy with sugar, spices, lemons and water mixed in. Nowadays, the combinations seem endless and very exotic. This mix of champagne and cooling fruit flavors makes a wonderful cocktail for a summer lunch.

1 (750 ml) bottle chilled champagne or dry sparkling white wine
4 cups / 750 ml chilled lemon-lime soda
5–6 tablespoons / 75 ml melon liqueur
5–6 tablespoons / 75 ml kiwi fruit liqueur
ice cubes
3 kiwi fruits, peeled and sliced, to decorate
1 piece water melon, deseeded and cut into balls, to decorate
lemon and lime peel twists and knots, to decorate

1. Pour the wine, soda and liqueurs into a large pitcher and stir gently; add plenty of ice cubes.
2. Decorate the pitcher with slices of kiwi fruit, melon balls and lemon and lime twists and knots. Serve in champagne flutes, spooning in a little of each fruit to decorate.

serves 6

Serenissima

This sophisticated cocktail based on vodka with grapefruit juice and Campari really does provide a feeling of calmness and relaxation—maybe that's where the name comes from.

1 measure vodka
1 measure grapefruit juice
1–2 dashes Campari
ice cubes

1. Put the vodka, juice and Campari into a cocktail shaker with a scoop of ice cubes.
2. Cover and shake vertically until the shaker is frosty, strain into a goblet half-filled with more ice cubes.

makes 1 cocktail

Caribbean Sunset

What could be better on a hot summer's evening than a cool cocktail with Caribbean flavors. A creamy mixture of gin, crème de banane, blue curacao and real fresh cream brings the cool Caribbean waters close to home.

1 measure gin
1 measure crème de banane
1 measure blue curacao
1 measure fresh whipping cream
1 measure lemon juice
splash of grenadine
ice cubes

1. Put the gin, crème de banane, blue curacao, cream and lemon juice into a cocktail shaker with a scoop of ice.
2. Cover and shake vertically until the shaker is frosty. Strain the cool blue mixture into a goblet and add a splash of grenadine.

makes 1 cocktail

Blue Lagoon

Close your eyes, take one sip of this refreshing vodka-based cocktail and you are on a deserted beach in Hawaii or Tahiti. This exotic blue cocktail really is as cooling as a Blue Lagoon.

1 ¹/₂ measures vodka
1 ¹/₂ measures blue curacao
chilled lemon-lime soda
ice cubes
cocktail cherries to decorate

1. Half fill a long stemmed goblet with ice cubes, pour in the vodka and curacao; stir gently.
2. Top off with the lemon-lime soda. If you like, decorate with a skewer of cocktail cherries.

makes 1 cocktail

Rosehip Tea & Strawberries

This fresh-tasting caffeine-free drink can be made with a herbal tea bag, available in most supermarkets. This cool combination makes a great alcohol-free summer cocktail.

decorate with a few rose petals or a tiny rose bud.

serves 4

4 rosehip and hibiscus tea bags
1 quart / 1 litre boiling water
8 oz / 250g fresh strawberries, hulled and
**   quartered**
ice cubes
strawberry slices and fresh rose petals, to
**   decorate**

1. Put the tea bags in a non-corrosive teapot or heat-proof pitcher. Pour over about 1 quart (1 litre) boiling water and allow to infuse about 15 minutes. Remove the tea bags, cool the tea and stir in the quartered strawberries. Refrigerate until chilled.
2. Fill highball glasses with ice cubes and strawberry pieces. Pour in the chilled tea and

Chapter Eight
Thanksgiving

Thanksgiving Bowl

This delicious cranberry-based fruit punch makes an ideal start to a traditional Thanksgiving dinner.

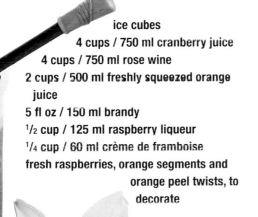

ice cubes
4 cups / 750 ml cranberry juice
4 cups / 750 ml rose wine
2 cups / 500 ml freshly squeezed orange juice
5 fl oz / 150 ml brandy
¹/₂ cup / 125 ml raspberry liqueur
¹/₄ cup / 60 ml crème de framboise
fresh raspberries, orange segments and orange peel twists, to decorate

1. Fill a large punchbowl about one third full with ice, then add all the ingredients except the garnish. Stir well and leave for 30 minutes before serving to allow the flavors to blend.

2. Before serving, add the fresh raspberries, orange segments and twists of orange peel and stir again to distribute evenly. If you like, float a few flowers on the surface. Using a ladle, pour into champagne flutes.

serves 8–10

Americano

When cocktails first came to Italy, they were all called Americanos because they were so strongly associated with America. This particular Americano is a long-time favorite cocktail.

ice cubes
1 measure Campari
1 measure sweet (red) vermouth
soda water
orange slice, lime slice and cocktail cherry, to decorate

1. Fill a glass with ice and pour in the Campari and vermouth. Stir in the soda water to taste.
2. Skewer an orange slice and lime slice with a cocktail cherry in the center on to a cocktail stick and rest on the edge of the glass.

makes 1 cocktail

Sloe Gin Fizz

Sloe gin is a delicious liqueur made from the bitter juices of sloes (the berries of the blackthorn bush) and sweetened gin. The most popular brand which has been around for over a century is Hawkers "Pedlar", although in Britain sloe gin is often made at home when the sloes are in season. In America, sloe gins include Leroux and Arrow.

1 1/2 measures sloe gin
juice of 1 freshly squeezed lemon
1 teaspoon superfine (caster) sugar
ice
soda water
lemon peel, to decorate

1. Pour the sloe gin, lemon juice and sugar into a highball glass and stir to dissolve the sugar.
2. Add ice and top up with soda water to taste. If you like, decorate with a long twist of lemon peel.

makes 1 cocktail

Hot Apple Pie Punch

This hot punch is an ideal drink for the Thanksgiving holidays. Remember when heating alcohol, if you wish to retain its strength, do not allow it to boil. On the other hand, if you do want to lose some of the strength without losing the flavor, then allow it to boil.

4 oz / 125g golden raisins (sultanas)
$^1/_2$ cup /125 ml dark rum
1 quart / 1 litre dry cider
$^1/_2$ cup /125 ml calvados (apple brandy)
4 x 2-inch / 5 cm pieces of cinnamon stick
16 whole cloves
1 apple, cored and thinly sliced

1. Put the golden raisins (sultanas) in a cup and cover with the rum, allow to soak for 2 hours.
2. Pour the dry cider and calvados into a large saucepan and add the soaked golden raisins (sultanas), cinnamon sticks and cloves, and heat very slowly; do not allow to boil. Pour into a large heatproof bowl or pitcher, and stir in the apple slices.
3. To serve, ladle the punch into heatproof glasses, making sure each glass has a few sultanas, cinnamon stick, cloves and apple slices.

4–6 servings

Chapter Nine
Halloween

Witches' Brew

This powerful cocktail gets its name from one of its main ingredients, strega liqueur. An Italian liqueur named after an ancient coven of witches who drank it as a love potion, strega consists of over 70 herbs. Combined with brandy and orange juice, it makes a great choice for a Halloween cocktail.

2 medium/large oranges
1 measure brandy, plus extra for lighting
1 ¹/₂ measures strega liqueur
fresh orange juice
cracked ice
a sprig of fir and kumquat faces, to decorate

1. Cut a quarter off the top of each orange and scoop out the orange flesh. Invert the small section into the bottom of the larger one, thus lining the bottom.
2. Pour a little of the extra brandy into the orange and, swirling and tilting the orange, use a long match to set light to the brandy. This will give a burnt-orange aroma that will permeate the cocktail.
3. Mix the brandy and strega in a mixing glass or measuring pitcher. Half fill each orange with ice and pour in the mixture. If you like, decorate with a sprig of fir tree and kumquat faces on skewers or cocktail sticks.

Tip: To follow the Halloween theme, use a sharp knife to carve little pumpkin faces into the kumquats as a finishing touch.

makes 1 cocktail

Zombie

This stunning cocktail is made from Opal Aera, or black sambuca, an Italian liqueur tasting of liquorice and elderberry. The wonderful intense color of black sambuca comes from distilling the purple-black elderberries with an infusion of aniseed, lemons and elderflowers, the recipe still a closely guarded secret.

ice cubes
1 measure Opal Aera
soda water or elderflower
  "champagne"
lemon peel knot

1. Half fill a champagne tulip with ice cubes.
2. Pour the Opal Aera over the ice and top with soda water or elderflower "champagne". Stir once and drop in a lemon peel knot and serve with a straw.

makes 1 cocktail

Bloodshot

This vodka-based cocktail is similar to a Bloody Mary, but oddly enough, contains beef bouillon (beef stock). Use extra Worcestershire sauce and Tabasco (chili sauce) if you like a very spicy drink. To make a Bullshot cocktail, leave out the tomato juice.

2 measures vodka
¹/₄ cup / 60 ml beef bouillon
** (beef stock)**
3 fl oz / 90 ml tomato juice
dash of freshly squeezed lime
** or lemon juice**
dash of Worcestershire sauce
dash of Tabasco sauce (chili
** sauce)**
freshly ground black pepper
celery salt
ice cubes
lime slices and two
** cherry tomatoes**
** to decorate**

1. Put the vodka, beef bouillon (beef stock), tomato juice, lime or lemon juice, Worcestershire sauce and Tabasco sauce (chili sauce) in a cocktail shaker. Season with freshly ground black pepper and celery salt, to taste; add a scoop of ice.
2. Cover and shake vertically until the shaker is frosty. Strain into a highball glass half-filled with ice and garnish with a slice of lime sandwiched with 2 cherry tomatoes on a cocktail stick.

makes 1 cocktail

Golden Gleem

This brandy-based cocktail takes on an orange flavor and glow from that sophisticated and greatest of the orange liqueurs, Grand Marnier—perfect for a Halloween cocktail.

1 measure brandy
1 measure Grand Marnier
$1/2$ measure freshly squeezed lemon juice
$1/2$ measure freshly squeezed orange juice
ice cubes
orange or lemon peel, to decorate

1. Put the brandy, Grand Marnier, and lemon and orange juices into a cocktail shaker with a scoop of ice.
2. Cover and shake vertically; strain into a wine goblet.

makes 1 cocktail

Chapter Ten

Christmas/Winter Holidays

Ross Royale

This brandy-based cocktail contains a rich crème de banane and the Royal Mint Chocolate liqueur which was invented in London by Peter Hallgarten. Hallgarten's is a respected London wine merchants, specializing in German wines. Deciding to branch out, Hallgarten developed Royal Mint Chocolate liqueur, the first new British true liqueur for many years, and one which is still a winner!

1 measure brandy
1 measure crème de banane
1 measure Royal Mint Chocolate liqueur
ice cubes

1. Put the brandy and liqueurs in a cocktail shaker with a scoop of ice.
2. Cover and shake vertically until the shaker is frosty. Strain into a cocktail glass.

makes 1 cocktail

Glühwein

Glühwein is the traditional Christmas drink in Germany and Austria. Glasses of this hot, cheering brew are sold from stalls in Christmas markets and town squares. A spiced hot wine fortified with brandy and rum, it makes a perfect choice for a Christmas party at home.

1 lemon, cut into six slices
18 whole ice cubes
36 fl oz / 1.4 litres red wine
¹/₂ cup / 125 ml brandy
3 tablespoons dark rum
5 oz / 150g light brown sugar
1 cinnamon stick
lemon slices and cinnamon sticks, to
  decorate

1. Spike each lemon slice with three cloves. Put them into a large, non-corrosive saucepan and add the wine, brandy, rum, sugar and cinnamon stick.
2. Slowly heat until the mixture begins to simmer, remove from the heat and allow to stand for at least 20 minutes.
3. To serve, reheat to the simmering point and ladle into heatproof punch glasses or goblets, floating a clove-studded lemon slice in each glass.

serves 6

Après Ski

This vodka-based drink couldn't be more refreshing. Cool crème de menthe, aniseed-flavored Pernod and lemon soda give a sophisticated twist to this gorgeous cocktail.

1 measure vodka
1 measure green crème de menthe
1 measure Pernod
ice cubes
chilled lemon soda
lemon slices and mint sprigs for garnish

1. Put the vodka, crème de menthe and Pernod into a cocktail shaker with a scoop of ice.
2. Cover and shake vertically until the shaker is frosty. Strain into a highball glass and top up with lemon soda. Decorate with a slice of lemon and a sprig of mint.

makes 1 cocktail

Spiced Tea

A perfect non-alcoholic drink on a cold winter's night. For an unusual twist, chill and serve with ice and orange peel.

4 cups / 1 litre water
3-inch / 7.5cm cinnamon stick
1-inch / 2.5cm piece fresh ginger root, peeled and sliced
$1/2$ teaspoon ground cardamom
10 black peppercorns
$1/2$ teaspoon ground cloves
coriander
4 tea bags
1 cup milk
honey or sugar, to taste

1. Put the water in a large saucepan and add the cinnamon, ginger, cardamom, peppercorns, cloves and coriander. Bring to a boil over medium-high heat, then simmer about 20 minutes. 2. Add the teabags and milk and simmer 5 more minutes; do not allow to boil once the milk has been added. Remove from the heat, sweeten to taste and serve hot in heatproof glasses.
3. Alternatively, refrigerate until chilled, serve over ice and decorate with a twist of orange peel.

serves 4

Chapter Eleven
Canapés and Snacks

Camembert baked in a box

This delicious idea is ideal for a small group of people who can gather round the plate and dip breadsticks, crackers and raw vegetables into the warm, gooey cheese. Ideal with wine/brandy-based cocktails, a small brie could be used with equal success.

**1 whole ripe but reasonably firm Camembert,
  in a box**
1 clove garlic, halved
a little fruity wine
grissini and/or crudités, to serve

1. Preheat the oven to 400F / Gas 6 / 200C.
2. Remove cheese from box and discard the wrapping. Return cheese to the box.
3. Rub cut sides of garlic over top of cheese. With a sharp knife, slice top off Camembert then replace it on top of cheese.
4. Pierce 6 holes in top of cheese with a skewer and trickle in a few drops of wine. Replace lid of box.

5. Bake cheese for 25–30 minutes, or until hot and bubbling. Remove lid and top slice of cheese. Place box of cheese on a plate and surround with grissini and/or crudités. Serve immediately while cheese is melted and runny.

Serves 6-8

Parmesan Crisps

These sophisticated rounds have a strong flavor which stands up to the most powerful cocktail. If you find all Parmesan cheese too expensive, use half Parmesan and half Romano, another Italian grating cheese.

melted butter for greasing
8oz / 225g Parmesan cheese, finely grated
2 tablespoons very finely chopped fresh
  chives

1. Preheat oven to 400F / Gas 6 / 200C.
2. Cover baking sheets with non-stick parchment / baking paper. Sprinkle cheese in mounds on baking sheets and flatten slightly with a fork to 2in / 5cm rounds. Bake for 2 $^1/_2$ minutes.
3. Sprinkle Parmesan rounds with chives and bake for a further 30 seconds. Remove from the oven and leave for 2 minutes to crisp.
4. Using a metal palette knife, transfer to a wire rack to cool.

Makes about 16

Feta Fingers

These tasty canapés are made with phyllo (filo) pastry which makes them lighter and more delicate than other cheese straws. They are best served warm.

6oz / 175g feta cheese, crumbled
3oz / 85g chopped, fresh flat-leaf parsley
2oz / 50g chopped fresh dill
freshly ground black pepper

about 9oz / 250g of filo pastry
melted butter for brushing
sesame seeds and/or poppy seeds for
  sprinkling (optional)

1. Preheat oven to 400F / Gas 6 / 200C. Oil a baking sheet.
2. Mix feta cheese, parsley, dill and pepper. Working with 1 sheet of filo at a time (keep remaining sheets covered), cut into 5x8in / 12.5x20cm strips.
3. With short end of strip towards you, brush with melted butter. Cover with a second strip. Put a teaspoon of cheese mixture at bottom of strip. Fold in $^1/_4$in / 0.5cm along each side. Roll up.
4. Transfer to baking sheet, brush with melted butter and sprinkle with seeds. Repeat with remaining cheese mixture and pastry.
5. Bake for 10 minutes, or until crisp and golden. Serve warm.

Makes about 30

Smoked Salmon Sushi

These elegant little canapés make a stunning presentation. Using smoked salmon is the ideal solution for those too squeamish to eat raw fish.

2 sheets toasted nori seaweed
1 teaspoon wasabi powder or horseradish
  cream
$^1/_2$ oz / 15g pickled ginger
6oz / 175g sliced smoked salmon
$^1/_4$ cucumber, cut into matchsticks
Japanese soy sauce for dipping
SUSHI RICE
6oz / $^3/_4$ cup / 175g Japanese rice
3 tablespoons rice vinegar
1in / 2.5cm piece kelp (optional)
pinch of sugar
salt

1. To prepare sushi rice, put rice, vinegar, kelp, and 9fl oz / 1 cup plus 2 tablespoons / 250ml water in a saucepan.
2. Cover and simmer until water has evaporated. Leave, still covered, for 10 minutes.
3. Discard kelp, and season with sugar and salt. Lay a nori sheet on baking parchment / greaseproof paper.

4. Spread a thin layer of rice to 3 edges but leave 2in / 5cm clear at far edge. Sprinkle with wasabi, or spread with horseradish. Arrange line of ginger across near edge, then top with salmon slice and a few sticks of cucumber.
5. Using baking parchment / greaseproof paper, roll up sushi to a tight cylinder. Leave to set for 1 hour. With a very sharp knife, cut into $^1/_2$in / 1cm slices. Serve with a small bowl of soy sauce.

Makes about 20

Pork Nuggets

These tasty morsels of marinated pork have a distinctly South-East Asian flavor and would make a tasty accompaniment to more exotic cocktails which have a sweeter, fruitier edge.

1 ³/₄ lb / 800g boneless lean pork, cut into
   1in / 2.5cm cubes
1oz / 25g cilantro / coriander leaves
3 cloves garlic, peeled
1 ¹/₄ in / 3cm piece of fresh root ginger, sliced
1 lemon grass stalk, outer layers removed
grated rind of 1 lime
large bunch of scallions / spring onions
2 large fresh red chilies, deseeded
2 tablespoons soy sauce
2 tablespoons clear honey
2 tablespoons white wine vinegar
2 tablespoons Thai fish sauce
2 tablespoons sesame oil
14fl oz / 400ml can coconut milk
lime wedges, to serve

1. Put pork in shallow non-metallic dish. Place half the coriander, garlic, ginger, 1 ¹/₄in / 3cm lemon grass, lime rind, and remaining ingredients except coconut milk in a blender and process finely.

2. Scrape over pork and stir to coat thoroughly. Cover and refrigerate overnight.

3. Remove pork from marinade; thread 2 cubes of pork on each wooden toothpick / cocktail stick. Reserve marinade. Preheat broiler / grill. Broil / grill pork nuggets for 4-5 minutes a side, brushing occasionally with some of the marinade.

4. Meanwhile, scrape remaining marinade into a skillet / frying pan, add coconut milk and remaining lemon grass. Chop remaining cilantro / coriander and add to sauce with any remaining marinade.

Makes about 30

Walnut Bread, Ham & Salsa

These delicious little open sandwiches make a slightly more substantial canapé. The nutty flavor of walnut bread also goes very well with goat's cheese which could be used as a vegetarian option.

1 loaf walnut bread, cut into $^1/_2$ in / 1cm slices
2 tablespoons olive oil
6oz / 175g ham, cut off the bone into 15 slices
2oz / $^1/_2$ cup / 50g walnuts, lightly toasted and finely chopped
fresh parsley or basil, to garnish
SALSA VERDE
3 tablespoons each chopped mint, cilantro / coriander and basil
1 clove garlic, chopped
2 tablespoons Dijon mustard
2 anchovy fillets
1 tablespoon capers
2fl oz / $^1/_4$ cup / 50ml olive oil
juice of $^1/_2$ lemon

1. To make salsa verde put all the ingredients into a blender and mix until smooth. Cover and chill.
2. Preheat broiler / grill. Brush bread slices with oil. Put under broiler / grill for about 1 minute or until lightly toasted.
3. Place a slice of ham on each piece of toast. Top with a spoonful of salsa verde then sprinkle chopped walnuts over. Garnish with basil or parsley.

Makes 15–30

Eggplant (Aubergine) Baskets

These pretty little baskets are easy to assemble at the last minute. Prepare the eggplant (aubergine) mixture, even a day ahead, but bring to room temperature, then spoon into the poppadum "baskets" just before serving.

2 large eggplants / aubergines
3 cloves garlic, crushed
1 $\frac{1}{2}$ tablespoons lime juice
2 teaspoons ground cumin

3 tablespoon chopped fresh cilantro / coriander
3 tablespoons olive oil
8 sundried tomatoes, drained and chopped
16 pitted black olives, finely chopped
freshly ground black pepper
1 packet mini poppadums, about 40
cilantro / coriander sprigs, and paprika (optional), to garnish

1. Preheat oven to 400F / Gas 6 / 200C.
2. Cut several slits in eggplants / aubergines then bake for about 1 hour or until very soft. Allow to cool. Cut eggplants / aubergines open, scoop out flesh and wrap in a clean cloth. Squeeze hard to remove moisture.
3. Mash eggplants / aubergines well with garlic, lime juice, cumin and cilantro / coriander. Stir in olive oil, sundried tomatoes and olives. Season with black pepper.
4. Spoon into the poppadums and garnish with cilantro / coriander sprigs, and paprika.

Makes 40

Nut & Coffee Meringues

Sometimes something sweet is the ideal finish for a cocktail party and a good signal that the party is over! Meringues don't like moisture, so make sure all your utensils are dry, and avoid making them on a humid day.

2 egg whites
4oz / $^1/_2$ cup / 115g superfine (caster) sugar
2oz / $^1/_2$ cup / 50g ground walnuts
chocolate-coated coffee beans, and pecan halves, to decorate
FILLING
about 7fl oz / scant 1 cup / 200ml heavy / double cream
about 1 tablespoon confectioners' / icing sugar, sifted
about 1 tablespoon espresso coffee powder

1. Preheat oven to 250F / Gas $^1/_2$ / 120C and cover baking sheets with baking parchment.
2. Whisk egg whites until stiff. Gradually add sugar, whisking constantly, and continue to whisk until mixture is very stiff and shiny. Gently fold in ground walnuts.
3. Spoon into pastry / piping bag fitted with nozzle, and pipe about 45 small discs of meringue on the baking sheets. Bake for about 1 hour until dry, very lightly colored and can be lifted easily from the baking parchment. Cool on wire rack.
4. To make filling, whip cream with sugar and coffee to taste. Just before serving, pipe a small swirl of cream on each base. Decorate some with chocolate-coated coffee beans and some with pecan halves. Serve in small paper cases.

Makes about 45

Index